I0477744

The Outsourcing Junkie

Getting Things Done with Fiverr

A Book on Saving Time and Money by Outsourcing
Simple Tasks

Jelani Copemann

Lab172 Publishing

Special Sales

Official print copies of The Outsourcing Junkie are available at special discounts for bulk purchase for sales promotions and premiums. For more information, please contact Special Sales, lab172publishing@gmail.com.

The Outsourcing Junkie: Getting Things Done with Fiverr

Table of Contents

Introduction

This book is intended to provide useful information for individuals who have never heard of Fiverr before and for those who may have heard about Fiverr but may not know of all the advantages that outsourcing tasks to freelancers on Fiverr can offer. These may include Businesses, Government & Private Agencies, Organizations, Parents, Entrepreneurs, Startups, Authors, Educators, Bloggers, Internet Marketers, Indie App Developers, Musicians, Promoters, Creatives and much more!

Intended to be used as a guide, this book was put together from multiple sources including, but not limited to, real-life case studies, interviews, online forums, websites, blogs, podcasts, etc. With this information, the idea was to organize everything into one simple, easy to read and relatable guide in which readers'

- Can learn and understand how the outsourcing process works
- Understand the benefits of outsourcing on Fiverr
- How to find the top Fiverr sellers on the platform
- How to grow your business with a virtual outsourcing team
- and much more

Creating my blog Lab172.com in 2014 opened the door to many new opportunities, new people and lots of information that I was not aware of at first. One of the main opportunities that I started to educate myself on was the practice of outsourcing small tasks and jobs to freelancers, particularly using online marketplaces like Fiverr. Today, I work with many freelancers on Fiverr to help me complete tasks related to my online businesses such as writing articles, illustrations, mobile app development and a few other tasks. The thing is, I've always thought that I would have to be at a certain level within my business or even have a lot of money to hire a freelancer, so I continued growing and building. Then something happened....

The main goal of Lab172.com is not only to document my journey of content creation and building online income, it also serves as a platform to a growing portfolio of projects and businesses that includes niche sites, blogs, mobile apps, a t-shirt line and more. A portfolio that is what I like to consider, "A work in progress." As with all internet marketers, bloggers, content creators, etc., one major aspect of this type of work is Time. There's lot of time and effort that is spent doing research and writing articles, building out sites and blogs, marketing content on social media and other platforms and other tasks that can really be time consuming.

If you are a one-man show, these are just some of the tasks that will require lots of time and energy from you in order for your business to run successfully. My first blog was an entertainment site about upcoming concerts, tours and live shows of musicians, comedians, and other forms of live entertainment. Before I even started on the site, I knew it would require lots of work to build up an audience and rank well within the search engines. After several months down the road, I was able to build up a small following for the blog because of some techniques and processes I've learned from other related sites and bloggers. It was around that time that I began creating more unrelated sites and started experimenting more with creating online content. It was also around that time that I started to see that I was probably biting off more than I can chew. For the most part, as you start to scale up, you start to run into problems and as stated earlier, one of your biggest problems is going to be time.

Typically, if you are new to the world of niche sites, blogs, podcasting, writing books, etc., you are going to spend a large amount of time researching and learning in the ins and outs of doing things. Another large portion of your time if you are not already proficient in that field, will be, again, doing research and learning about the things in which you are either blogging about, writing reviews on a certain product for your niche sites or doing video courses and training. The reality of how much work, time, and energy that is REALLY required kicked in. What you essentially set out to do and the experience that you have in that field will ultimately dictate the difficulty level you will experience. Everyone learns in different ways and because I was engaging into something that I found fun and interesting, it made the learning curve a lot easier even though there were days that I was ready to give up.

From the beginning, my entire mind frame was that I would build these blogs and niche sites from the ground up myself with little to no money. I would then slowly but surely build up revenue to pay for the expenses of growing the sites. I started researching and learning from other bloggers and internet entrepreneurs and saw that they did the same thing and that there was something else they were doing that many of them had in common. Just like me, many of them started out as a one-man show, handling every aspect of running their online businesses, but as they started to scale up, they would hire Freelancers and Virtual Assistants s to handle certain tasks.

Seeing the success that many people have had by hiring a freelancer or a virtual assistant to complete certain tasks while they focus on the more critical aspects of their business was nothing new to me. What was new was seeing the new and improved marketplaces and platforms now available to offer services that came along as online technologies started to mature. The cost of providing services that were once only available to major companies has dramatically declined and are now available to anyone who needs them. You don't have to have a business in order to use a freelancer or a virtual assistant these days. Just about any task you have can be completed these days by hiring a freelancer or a VA.

I decided that if I am going to grow these sites and possibly take on other opportunities, I would need an efficient system in place that will allow me to scale at an efficient pace. Hiring a freelancer to help out with a few articles was a no-brainer because of all the advantages that come with it. One of the main advantages for me to outsource certain tasks is it not only gives me the opportunity to get things done but it allows me to get certain projects and tasks that I am not necessarily educated on or have the technical knowledge to complete. My first time outsourcing an entire project on Fiverr was not about articles but rather the development of a mobile puzzle game app. The process alone taught me critical fundamental knowledge that makes up the foundation of this book. Since then, I have been working with multiple freelancers on several different projects and have also been teaching many friends and associates how they can use Fiverr for some of their business needs and day to day tasks.

Fiverr is only one of several marketplaces where you can easily hire a freelancer to assist you with your projects and tasks, but it has been one of my most useful tools that I constantly use time and time again. There're thousands of creative individuals that are held back from going after the things they love to do because they may not have the necessary knowledge or skills to complete their projects. I strongly feel that if more people knew how easy it is to outsource certain tasks and projects, more individuals would start building, creating and pursuing their dreams.

Chapter 1. What is Outsourcing

The term "outsourcing" was a term typically used throughout many industries within the business world. While you will find different definitions worded differently, the basic principles of outsourcing are the same across the board. In short, the word outsourcing can be defined as a practice in which an individual or company performs tasks, provides services or manufactures products for another company -- functions that could have been or is usually done in-house. Outsourcing is also referred to as "contracting out" by many people. To look at it in one perspective, if you have ever paid someone to do a service or make a product for you, technically you have used the basic principles of outsourcing.

A Brief History of Outsourcing

In the early 1990's, organizations began to use the advantages of outsourcing in an effort to focus more on cost-saving measures that will increase their markets and their profits. As the process started to evolve, companies of all sizes started to outsource more functions necessary to run a company but not related specifically to the core business. Departments, functions, and tasks such as accounting, human resources, data processing, internal mail distribution, security, lawn maintenance and more became commonly outsourced jobs.

This alone has left thousands of skilled workers without a job and on the other end, allowed thousands of the same individuals to start their own business by becoming a contractor or freelancer that companies hire when they are looking to outsource internal projects. In more recent times, the innovation of technology has opened up the practice to just about anyone who is skilled in a certain area and would like to sell their services as a full-time business or for extra income. It has also opened up the practice to not only smaller size companies, but also to individuals who are looking for someone skilled in a particular area to complete certain tasks. Whether you're a new startup company looking for someone to create a logo or you are someone looking for professional advice, tips, and private lessons, virtually anyone can now hire freelancers or contractors to complete tasks for them. Also, with all of the new marketplaces for creative and professional services that are now available online, the cost of outsourcing had dramatically lowered compared to the cost several years ago, when it was once only affordable to large companies and certain individuals.

Who are the Parties Involved in the Outsourcing Process?

During the outsourcing process, there're 3 parties involved. There's the buyer of the services/product and there's the provider of the services/product. The third, which has become increasingly popular in recent times, is the marketplace in which the buyer and the service providers meet in order to do business. The buyers of the services can range from large companies to individuals who may need certain services or tasks to be done. The service providers are usually freelance professionals or contractors who are knowledgeable and experts in a certain field. These fields can range from editors, illustrators, apps, and website developers, songwriters and more. The marketplaces are generally websites that match buyers and sellers of services/products and are paid a percentage of each sale transaction. Websites like Fiverr, Upwork, 99Designs, Elance, Guru, and Peopleperhour are some of the top freelance marketplaces that offers thousands of services for any project needs.

While the terms "freelance" and "contractors" can be used interchangeably, there are some differences between the two. The term Freelance, which will be the term used throughout the book, refers to self-employed individuals who are skilled in certain areas, hired by clients for a short duration project and are paid a fixed amount to do a defined job. The term contractors refer to individuals who are usually "contracted" for a certain amount of time on projects that have longer durations and generally are required to work at the client's place of business. Both terms are similar in that the individuals are experts in their fields and are only committed to a project for a certain duration. However, some common qualities and differences separates the two.

Common Qualities of a Freelancer

- Works from home, office or at their choice of location
- Self Employed, works independently and are not committed to any long-term employment
- Determines the rate at which they are paid and are responsible for handling their own prices, taxes, legal paperwork, etc.
- Typically works on multiple, smaller projects with a shorter time frame
- Commonly used in the culture and creative industries such as music, writing, acting, computer programming, web design, translation, etc.

Common Qualities of a Contractor

- May work as a sub-contractor under a larger contracting company
- Usually works on site or at a job specific location
- Typically works on larger projects with a longer time frame ranging from 1-12+ months
- Usually are paid an hourly rate or a fixed rate from their company.
- Commonly used in the industrial sectors which includes IT Professional Services, Property Maintenance, Construction, Waste Management, Aerospace, and Defense, etc.

Common Qualities of a Freelance Marketplace

- Traditionally has thousands of highly skilled professionals, experts, and skilled freelancers within the marketplace and their community blogs and forums sites
- Makes money by charging a fixed rate or a percentage of each sale transaction
- Allows sellers or service providers to create a sellers' profile allowing them to show their description, rates, examples of their work along with access to a management dashboard for sales and traffic data. Buyers can create a buyers' profile which allows them to create simple profiles, post requirements for project tasks and access to a management dashboard to track ongoing projects.
- May operate as a bidding platform marketplace where buyers bid on a price for a certain service, or they may operate as an open platform marketplace in which the seller determines their prices.

- Message boards which allows buyers and sellers to network and communicate with each other privately

The entire outsourcing process and the parties involved have and still are changing the way companies and individuals are doing business, projects and day to day tasks. It offers many advantages to companies and individuals that are looking for knowledge and expertise in a certain field, as well as to people who are looking to use their knowledge to make a living as a freelancer.

Chapter 2. Advantages of Outsourcing

Depending on the many factors like the type of tasks being outsourced, the type of business you may have and other factors will depend on the benefits you will see from the outsourcing process. However, there's several advantages and benefits that are the top driving force which attracts most individuals to hire a freelancer to handle certain functions of their projects.

Low Cost Services

This is the most popular reason why companies and individuals hire freelancers. For example, you can get a highly specialized task completed for a small fraction of what it would normally cost you from a freelancer on Fiverr. If you have a task that needs to be completed but you may not be skilled enough to complete the task, you can find a freelancer on Fiverr who can do the job on a relatively small budget. There are tons of people on Fiverr with the specialized skill-set that can get the certain jobs done at a fraction of the cost it would normally cost by hiring a consulting agency.

Cost Savings Opportunities

To go along with the advantage that is listed above, when you hire a freelancer, you never have to worry about putting them on your payroll. Instead of having to hire an employee and add them to your monthly payroll, you can simply set your terms up front with your service provider. In addition to not having to add a new employee to your payroll, outsourcing also allows you to save money on benefits. If you hire a new employee you will more than likely have to offer them a wide range of benefits, which can cut into your profits over time. But when you outsource a project you will never have to worry about benefits because the person you are hiring will be a freelancer.

Specialized Skills

This brings us to another point. You can obtain specialized help via Fiverr for numerous tasks such as voice-overs, animation, illustrations, building websites, creating SEO optimized content or completing some basic functions of a project – whatever task a project requires, you can find a freelancer on Fiverr to do for you. On top of finding specialized freelancers to handle certain tasks, utilizing someone else's skills allows you to free up precious time so that you can focus on other things that you are more versed in.

Focus on the Big Picture

When you are just starting up or running a company or you have a project that you are working on, it demands a lot of your time, energy and efforts. Although every detail of the project is important, there're usually a few minor tasks that you don't want to spend too much time on because of its' level of importance. Also, you may not have the manpower to tackle certain things. Outsourcing these little tasks to freelancers will help you stay focused on the important and bigger goals. You will be freeing up much-needed bandwidth so you can focus on things like creating new products, networking, finding new accounts, funding, etc. You can hire one or several freelancers to handle smaller tasks like your social media accounts, emails, and other small tasks.

Flexibility

Managing a project or even running a business can sometimes consume your life and energy, taking you away from your personal life for long periods at a time. You seem to be working day in and day out, sometimes without a single day off. Hiring someone to take over some menial task could free up some time for you to take a much-needed break; which is important if you are working 18 hours each day. Working all the time can zap the creativity out of you. You do need some personalized time to unwind and allows more new ideas to come in. This is also very helpful when you have a project that pops up out of nowhere and you need immediate assistance. It allows you the flexibility to always have an extra helping hand when you need one, but without ever having to directly hire them as a permanent employee.

Improved Services

Let's say that you run a home business and you have a service or a product that may require customer support. What if you do not have the budget to hire a customer support team, which would also require training on product and customer support. If you are a one-man business, what if a client or customer requires support after normal business hours or at time when you are working on other tasks? These are some of the problems that can be solved by hiring virtual assistant or a freelance customer support rep on Fiverr. You can find lots of individuals with type of skills and knowledge you will need especially if customer service is not your strength. Now, we are not talking about just customer service but other functions as well such as web content, product packaging and many more. Even if you know how to do the task, you may even get a better product or service if you outsource it to Fiverr. This will provide you with the time to focus on building the brand instead.

Chapter 3. What is Fiverr

Now, I know I've partially explained a little about the Fiverr marketplace, but in this chapter, we will go into further details about what Fiverr really is, how it's different from other marketplaces,

Fiverr is a global online marketplace offering tasks and services, beginning at a cost of $5 per gig performed. The Services called 'gigs" offered on the site includes writing, translation, graphic design, video editing, animation, programming and more. Fiverr is the world's largest marketplace for creative and professional services, currently listing over 3 million Gigs in more than 100 different categories across 196 countries. The site is primarily used by freelancers who uses Fiverr to offer their services to customers worldwide, whether it is businesses or individuals.

How Does Fiverr Work

Fiverr offers a very easy-to-use platform that works well for both those wishing to offer services and those who wish to purchase services. Anyone wishing to utilize Fiverr as either a seller or a buyer, must first register for an account which is completely free of charge.

As a buyer, you can browse the different categories and subcategories on Fiverr or can simply use their "Search Box" to find the services you're looking for. As you are doing your search, you will have access to the details of each seller and their services such as the seller's description of the service, samples of that individual's work, and his/her Fiverr reviews made by previous buyers. If the service you are looking for is available, then you can instantly place an order for $5 and if it's not, then you can create a "Special Request" describing what you want (with your budget and other requirements) so that the Fiverr community can create a custom gig or offer for you.

Just make sure that you're buying only from credible sellers who have a good track-record. You can check the rating, feedback, average response time, and the current portfolio of all sellers to assess the quality of their services. And it's a good idea to contact the seller before you purchase a Gig to make sure that they can deliver what you want.

Examples of Fiverr Gigs

So you can get a better understanding of what a "Gig" is and how they appear on the Fiverr platform, here is an example of some gigs being offered under the "Writing & Translation" category.

Figure 1

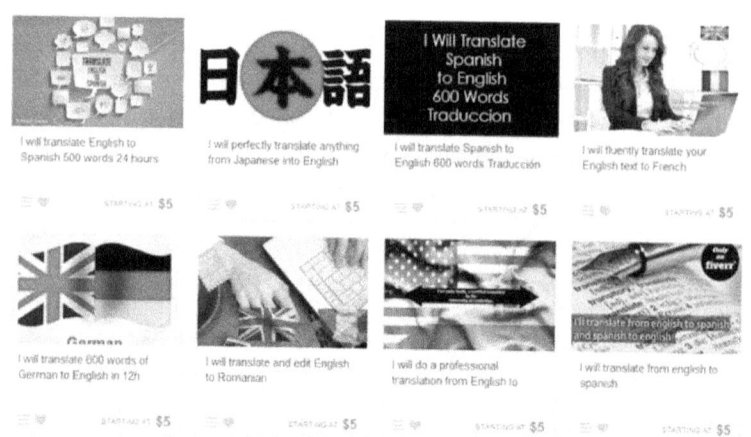

As you can see in Figure 1, there're many Gigs offering translation services such as English to Spanish, Japanese to

English, English to French and so on. Just by looking at some of the different services, you can get a short description of the services that are being offered and the starting price.

Now clicking on one of the gigs, in this case, we used the first gig in Figure 1, you will get a more detailed description of the what is being offered.

Figure 2

About This Gig

What we Offer:

We will translate up to 500 words in less than 24 hours.
All members of our team are native Spanish speakers, with extensive translation experience of various types of materials.
We do not use any kind of translating software, which ensures a quality work.

We offer a 100% satisfaction guarantee, you will be able to make UNLIMITED revisions to the translated material
and if you are still not satisfied with the our work, we will refund your money.
Our customer service team is online 24/7.
Once we delivere the finished work, feel free to request any number of changes and we'll modify your text

Summary:

- Human Translation, Not Software guarantee.
- Team of Native Spanish Speakers.
- All kinds of material accepted.
- 24/7 Customer Service.
- 100% satisfaction guaranteed or money back.
- Proofreading in translation.

Languages
English
to Spanish

Figure 2, shows a more detailed description of the gig, which is offering to translate 500 words from English to Spanish in 24 hours for $5. When you look a little lower, you will see more details of the gig such as the info on the team providing the translation services, their availability, the revisions and refund policy and everything else that you will be receiving for $5. On the corner, there's the order button, ability to change the quantity of gigs you are paying for, a section to share the gig on social media, and additional information about the seller like their location, their seller rating, the language that they speak, etc. This is the basic format that you will find on Fiverr when you are searching through different gigs. However, there're thousands of different gigs on Fiverr, so each gig, even if it is for the same services, will differ from seller to seller.

Types of Gigs on Fiverr

When you got to the Fiverr Platform, you will notice that the platform is broke down into separate categories which allows you to make your search much easier. In all, there're about 12 main Categories which consists of Graphics & Design, Digital Marketing, Writing & Translation, Video & Animation, Music & Audio, Programming & Tech, Advertising, Business, Lifestyle, Gifts, Fun & Bizarre, and Other.

Under each of the 12 main categories, there're also tons of sub-categories, that lets you find specific services related to each main category. For example, under the Graphics & Design category, you will find subcategories such as services such as Logo Designs, Illustrations, Cartoons & Caricatures, Banner Ads, Flyers & Posters, Book Covers & Packaging and much more. Some of the subcategories under Music &

Audio consists of Voice Overs, Mixing & Mastering, Producers & Composers, Jingles & Drops, and more. Some of the more weird and uncommon services offered on Fiverr are under the Fun & Bizarre Category. Under this category, you will find subcategories such as Celebrity Impersonators, Daredevils & Stunts, "Your Message On" Advertising, Dancers, Pranks and other Bizarre services. With Fiverr, you will find just about any type of service you will need under one of the main categories available.

In Figure 3, you will find an example of some of featured Gigs on Fiverr. These Featured Gigs are usually some of the most popular Gigs on Fiverr and are from the top-rated sellers within the community. You will also get a glimpse of the different gigs offered on the platform such as

Figure 3

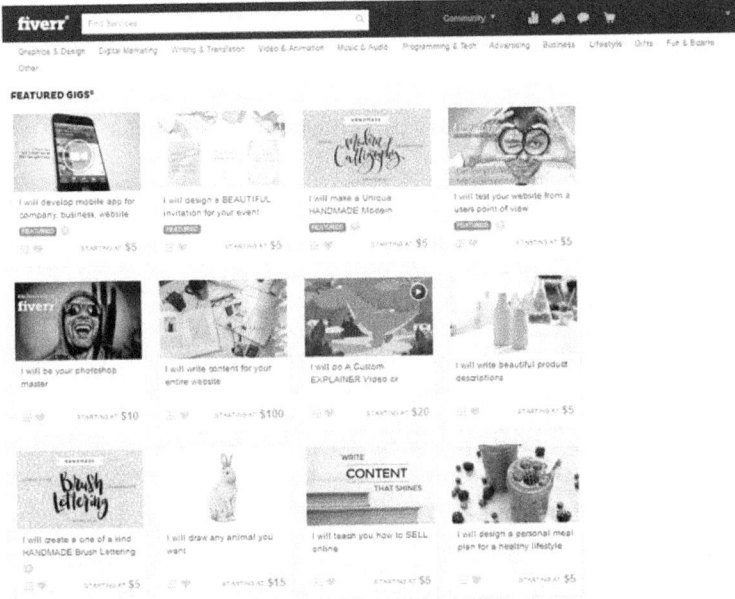

Custom Gigs, Add-Ons, and Gigs more than $5

One way for sellers to make additional income while providing additional services is to offer Add-Ons, Custom Gigs, and Gigs with more than one pricing level which are all known as "Gig Extras." These Gig Extras allow the buyers an opportunity to buy related services or add premium features. For example, if a seller is designing logos for $5, then you may get "Gig Add-Ons" like one-day delivery, multiple-file formats, business card designs that matches your new logo, multiple revisions, etc. Then there's another feature where you can also buy additional quantities (known as "Gig Multiples") from the seller if they are offering it. If the seller is offering "Gig Multiples" then you get a chance to buy 2 logos for $10. The Custom Order feature allows you to contact the seller with details about your order (or project) and request additional features that may not be offered with the gig or as a Gig Add-On. Custom orders gives the buyer the opportunity to customize the gig to fit your needs and also allow you to have a more flexible pricing for the additional features you are requesting for the Gig.

Now as you search through the different gigs, you will find that there're many gigs that cost more than $5 or may have more than one pricing level. Although all services on Fiverr has a base price of $5, top sellers often list their basic services for $10 or more. These top sellers are given the opportunity to sell their services at a higher cost because they have proven to be a reputable seller and will give you a higher quality of service. This is beneficial for both the buyers and sellers because often times, to offer a quality service for only $5 can sometimes make the Gigs too limited, preventing sellers from offering what they want, and prevented buyers from finding what they need. At the end of the day, most buyers are looking for a large range of services and are willing to pay substantially more to get exactly what they need which can be purchased using Extras, Multiples, and Custom Orders.

In Figure 4, you can examine an example of a gig that cost a little more than $5, has several price points and is offered by a top seller. In this particular Gig, the seller is offering to design a high-quality logo at 3 different price levels. The first price level starts at $30, which gives you 1 basic high-resolution logo with transparency, 1 logo design and up to 3 revisions. The next level for $50 which is their Premium Package, gives you 2 high resolution logo designs with transparency, a vector file and up to 9 revisions. The last and most expensive package for $80, gives you 3 of their best logo designs and all of the Add-On features which includes high resolution files, vector files, a 3D mockup of your logo, unlimited revisions, and the source file.

Keep in mind that while these top sellers are guaranteeing their best work for more money, many times you can find the same service with the same quality, for a lesser price. The key thing when purchasing Gigs on Fiverr is to do your research on the seller, their services and their quality of work.

Figure 4

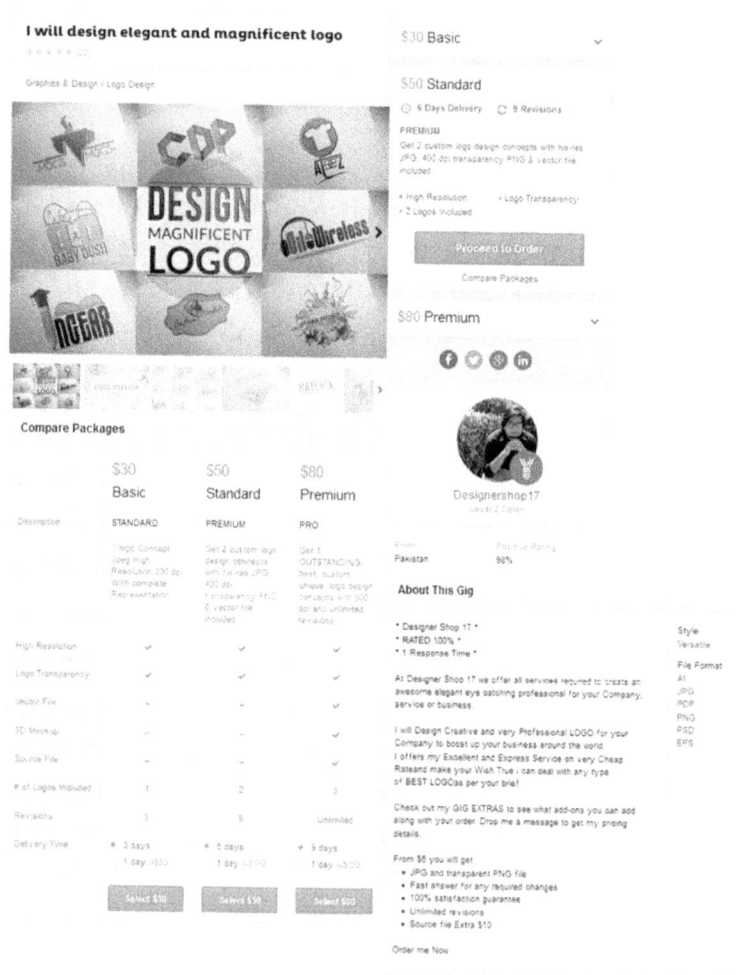

Chapter 4. Hiring a Freelancer on Fiverr for your Project

Now that there's a basic understanding of outsourcing and Fiverr, the next step would be to start the hiring process. Although you may not be hiring someone for a full-time position at a large company, you are still hiring someone to handle tasks that are just as important to your business and projects. And just like many of the processes that most company uses to recruit or hire individuals, you will need to employ some of those processes when searching through the different gigs. Choosing the gig and the freelancer doing the gig, overtime becomes an easy task once you get familiar with the Fiverr platform because the platform is already setup to promote the top gigs and its' freelancers. While utilizing their system, you will also need to have your own system to identify the best freelancers on the platform who can deliver exactly what you want. For me, I've come up with a simple system which starts by determining, research and assess, communication and purchasing.

Determining Your Project Needs

The first step starts by identifying the work in the project which you add the least value by doing yourself. This can also include things that you may not be knowledgeable on, qualified to do and even tasks that you may not have the available time to complete. Whatever task it is, you need to identify it and list all of its details, clarifying exactly what you need and the exact desired results for the task, your available budget to outsource the task and the delivery date you need for the outsourced work. Answering these questions beforehand will make the process so much easier because you are setting perimeters and guidelines for the task that can be used to keep yourself and the person you are hiring accountable throughout the process.

Researching & Assessing the Quality of a Gig

The next step, once you have figured out the task or project that is being outsourced is to start researching the different Gigs and assessing the quality of each one. As we talked about in the early chapters, looking through the platform for Gigs is very easy using the category list or the search bar. With the help of the seller ratings, you can easily conduct a quick research of a gig and the freelancer providing the gig. All you need to do is to check seller's profile and see the overall ratings and what other buyers thought about their service. Of course, if a seller is good at what he/she does, the ratings will speak for them. Poor sellers usually get poor ratings.

On top of the seller ratings, the Gig description will be clear and concise, getting straight to the point with what you are receiving and its' price but it is also common to have few questions about their services. Sellers with good profiles and gig descriptions are most likely to deliver the best work for your money.

Potential buyers are able to assess a seller's quality by the Fiverr reviews left by previous customers. Once a Gig has been completed successfully, buyers are able to rate a seller's level of quality on a scale of one to five stars, with one star representing poor quality of service and five representing excellent quality of service. The areas that sellers are rated on includes:

Custom Orders & Special Requests

As I've mentioned before, Fiverr has thousands of skilled and knowledgeable freelancers within the community. Many of these freelancers are also skilled in many other areas and sometimes may not post gigs for all of the services they can offer. With that being said, sometimes you may need a service for a project that is not listed on Fiverr or you may have trouble finding what you are looking for, and when that happens, you can then submit a Gig request or a custom order. The "Custom Order" feature allows you to contact a seller with a customize request of a Gig. For example, if there is a Gig that offers to do a video testimonial for you, you can request a custom order for that Gig for things like, a natural background, music playing in the background, a specific gender doing the testimonial, etc. When you request a custom order, the price of the Gig may increase to accommodate the additional requests.

To request a custom order, you would first find a Gig by browsing through the thumbnails on the homepage, category, or subcategory pages or you can visit a seller's profile page. Once you have found a Gig that you like, you will then click the thumbnail of the Gig you would like to order then proceed to the "Do you have any special requirements?" area, then click "Request a Custom Order." In that section, you will need to describe the service you are looking for and attach any files. This will help the seller cater to your specific request. You can also select the specific criteria for your order. For example, you can select gender, language, age range, purpose, accent, and so on. This is optional and varies based on the type of service you are looking for.

When you are using the "Request a Gig" feature, this allows you to make a request to the Fiverr community for a specific service that is not listed on Fiverr as a Gig. If your request meets certain criteria's of a seller, the seller will submit an offer. In your dashboard, you will need to go to the Request section then to 'Post a Request." In the description area, you will need to write specifically what you are searching for. For example, if you are looking for a logo, you can specify your company name, business type, preferred color, etc. If you want, you can attach a file.

If your request meets the criteria of a seller, the seller will submit an offer. Your request will only be shown to people who deliver work within the categories you've selected, and this will save you time. Fiverr only gives you 300 characters to post your request, so you want to be clear enough in your post that the right person will read it and know they can deliver the work, so that they send you an offer.

Communication with Multiple Freelancers

Something you will want to keep in mind after researching different Gigs is that you have options among the many Gigs available in each category. In order to hire the best freelancer for your project, you will want to contact multiple freelancers within the category you are researching. Each freelancer on Fiverr has a different style and way of doing things, so communicating with a few of them and having these options can help you choose the best one who can deliver exactly what you need and in the time frame you will be receiving the services.

Even if the service is as described in the Gig description, before you hire a freelancer on Fiverr, there are some basic questions you will want to ask so that you have a clear understanding of the overall details of the Gig. You will want to contact the Fiverr freelancer first to request for samples of previous works (proofs or examples), to confirm that freelancer's availability within the time-frame you want your job completed and depending on the type of project you are doing will dictate the more detail questions you will need to ask. For example, when I first set out to have a few mobile gaming apps built, the description was very clear on what I would be getting, but because there was some customization to the apps, the prices would increase. Also, I sent out 5 emails to 5 different freelance developers on Fiverr whose Gig description fit what I was trying to do. Once I communicated with the developers about what I wanted, they all sent back custom quotes, all more than $5. From there, I purchased the Gig that provided me with the best examples and prices. Communication is key when hiring Freelancers on Fiverr.

Chapter 5. Pricing and How to Negotiate

In Chapter four, we detailed the process of hiring a freelancer on Fiverr. This chapter focuses more strongly on how to set a budget for a project, as well as how to negotiate for a better deal.

The main thing to remember when you are dealing with the issue of cost is that you want to make sure that both sides are getting a fair deal. Also, as we talked about in previous chapters, all of the services on Fiverr has a base price of $5. It usually costs more add-ons, custom orders, and premium services, so anything outside of the basic services will cost you more money. A deal in which one side is getting a far better value is going to be doomed from the beginning. If the freelancer thinks that he or she is not getting paid enough, they will not give their best effort. This is why it is critical to get several quotes from different freelancers. You will have the ability to choose the service that you feel will provide the best quality and the best price that fits within your budget. Finding a happy medium that both sides can agree on is the best way to ensure a successful project for everybody that is involved. The tricky thing about cost, especially on Fiverr is that each side will have their own guidelines and rates that they are trying to follow. The tips below are meant to help you deal with prices discrepancies.

The first thing that both sides need to do is communicate on the budget for the project. In most cases, you can just go and purchase the advertised Gig for the basic price of $5 pay for add-ons or premium services. In other cases, when you have a custom order or special requests, the freelancer will issue you a custom quote that outlines the total cost of completing the project. This will allow the freelancer to start off within his or her price range, and also help you determine whether or not the total cost is within your budget.

After receiving your custom quotes, you can decide which will be accepted and rejected. If you agree to the terms that the freelancer outlines in the proposal everything is good to go. On the other hand, if the freelancer's price is higher than the budget will allow, you still have others to choose from and in some cases, you can send a counter offer. Now if it ever comes to the point where you will have to send a counteroffer to the freelancer, ultimately it will be up to him or her to decide if they can complete the project for that amount of money. However, it is not uncommon for the freelancer to send over another counteroffer as a way to finalize the deal with an offer that may be more appropriate for the amount offered.

When you are negotiating, keep these tips in mind:

- Keep an open mind. If you are looking to outsource a project you must realize that the freelancers, especially on Fiverr are professionals, and sometimes take on these projects to make a living. Generally speaking, they usually have a rating system that they follow in order to give accurate quotes to all of their prospective clients.
- Always stay professional during the negotiation process. If you do not agree with their quotes because their prices or description do not fit your needs, it is easier to explain your situation, and see if there is a compromise with counter offers that will make both

parties happy. And if nothing works out, you can easily walk away and find another freelancer that may be able to complete your project within your budget. Remember, this is a business for both parties involved. Each side needs to do what is best for them.

Chapter 6. A Short Fiverr Case Study

In this Chapter, you will be able to read a short case study that I've published on my blog, Lab172 detailing the entire process that I used to outsource the creation of my first few mobile apps to releasing them in Google Play App Store. The article, "How I Built My First Mobile Apps for $20 - A Fiverr Case Study" was a what I would refer to as a quick start guide to this book. The reason for this is because once you have read the entire article, you will have the basic understanding of how to outsource your own mobile apps and published them in the app stores. The thing is, it doesn't cover all of the unique aspects and the many different categories of services that is offered on the Fiverr platform by the thousands of freelance developers, artists, graphic designers, illustrators, etc.

How I Built My First Mobile Apps for $20 - A Fiverr Case Study

As there are thousands of apps on the market, there's even more being built and uploaded to app stores on a daily basis. Millions of people use apps every day to handle simple and complex tasks in their lives, play games and just about every possible activity you can do with a mobile phone, tablet, and a computer. What many people don't realize is that you can have your own app designed and built for little money. Now while it does take a lot more money to build a more detailed app, a simple game app like puzzle and word games or even wallpaper apps can be built for way less than you may think.

Learning The App Market

Before jumping into the mobile app world, you may want start learning about the different tools and services that you will need in order to get the app working. You will also need to learn about the different monetization methods, some of the different words and their meanings in the developer world, and other services and tools you would need to accomplish getting your app up and running in the app store. During my trial and error stages, I came across a book, "Mobile Apps Made Simple: The Ultimate Guide to Quickly Creating, Designing and Utilizing Mobile Apps for Your Business."

This is a great book and has been very helpful for me when I first started looking into having some mobile apps built for me since I knew nothing about coding and mobile app development. It is simply about setting up a plan and how to go about designing a mobile app on your own. It gives you a guide on how to start out planning for your app, software to program the apps, some of the programming languages that can be used, and other steps necessary in making your own app. It is really helpful for those with no technical skills who wishes to get a jump start with their app development. The idea behind the first apps came from watching some videos on YouTube by an online entrepreneur who was already established in the app market. She gives some great advice and tips in her videos about making money online, building your first app and getting it on the market to creating simple designs for Etsy and fulfillment sites like Zazzle and Cafepress. She also points out some of the problems you may encounter and how to go about solving them which were very similar to the things I encountered.

To start, you may want to get familiar with the online outsourcing marketplace Fiverr which is one of the top sites to get small tasks or jobs outsourced. You can get someone to write code, design graphics, build apps, websites and so much more and the best part about it is that all the services have a base price of $5. You can also get additional work and customization done by paying a little extra for their premium services. You can talk with different developers and see which one offers you the best deal and offers the best quality work. Listed below are some of my first apps that were published in the Google Play Store:

- Drain
- Animal Friends

These two mobile puzzle apps are my first apps that was built for the android market and was used as a test to see exactly how the whole process works using Fiverr and Google Play Store. I gained a lot of knowledge during the whole process as both apps were designed by 2 separate developers. One of the developers went a great deal in helping me get the app built, to uploading it to the app store and because he was so helpful and did not charge me for the extra work he did (which he had every right to), I now give him most of the jobs I need done for my mobile app portfolio.

Deciding on the type of App

As said above, some of the easiest and low-cost apps to build are usually puzzles, word games, and wallpaper apps. Normally, you might have to get the code, sounds and images separately especially if you are not designing the app 100% on your own, but many developers provide everything you may need except for images and sounds. Occasionally, the sounds may be included but for the most part, you will have to provide your own images. Getting your images is critical because you want to stand out from the hundreds of apps on the market and not have the same images as other related apps.

For some of my first few apps, I purchased images from the online micro-stock platform, Fotolia and used some free pics from Pixabay, a website for sharing royalty free and public domain images and film. You can find any type of images, vectors, icons from cartoons, vintage, nature, animals, etc. for free or for a low cost. The only problem with free images is that many people have already used them in their projects so the best option is using a service that gives you single or bulk images for a low set price.

I would also like to add that the mentioned above apps are not the only app you can have built for little money. After building relationships with some of the other developers on Fiverr, I came to realize that many of the developers may already have a generic game that can be customized with different graphics, sounds, and features so it can be sold to multiple people without anyone having the same looking game. I find these apps to be great for beginners due to the fact that your only responsibility is obtaining the small things like mentioned above (graphics, sounds, etc.)

One of the biggest questions you will also need to ask yourself is which platform will you be using to build and publish your apps on. You have a choice of many, but the top 4 are Google Play Store and Amazon App Store which are both android platforms, Apple App Store, and Microsoft Windows Market Place. Personally I use Google Play Store which I found a lot easier to use and cheaper on publishing costs. For a one-time $25 fee, I can publish as many apps as I want as long as it's free. If you want to sell priced apps, in-app products, or subscriptions, you'll need a Google Wallet Merchant Account.

Once my publishing account was set up, I went back to Fiverr to find a developer that can develop the type of app I wanted. I already knew what type of app I wanted to have built, so now I just needed someone to build it for me or purchase the generic coding to have it customized. With the first two apps, Chicken Hero & Friends and Animal Friends, the generic puzzle code was already in place and all I needed to provide the developers with was graphics. Once that was provided and the work was completed which only took a few days, they provided me with the.APK file, which stands for Android Application Package. The Android application package file (APK) is the file format used to distribute and install application software and middleware onto Google's Android operating system. It is the format used for Android mobile apps.

Monetizing the App

As I mentioned earlier, I am able to publish as many apps in the app store since I have paid the $25 registration fee, but the catch is that the apps has to be free to download. I can easily upgrade my account to do in-app purchases and paid apps but there are many reasons why it will be better off free. The first two apps are very basic apps and was created to test out the entire system so I would know what I am doing for my future apps I am planning on having outsourced. Although I will use them to test a few new features before applying them to other apps, it will be better to keep it free which also allows for more downloads. Also, due to the quality of those apps, it's not something I would be comfortable releasing at a cost.

Some of my other apps are a lot more detailed with original content and are on the market as free apps also but for the most part, unless it is a highly expensive app I am outsourcing, all of my apps will be for free to download. Currently, the only form of monetization I use are "in-app" ads. There are a few mobile advertising programs you can sign up with, like *AdMob*, which allows you to generate a code, place the code in the app file, and make money once someone clicks on the ads that are shown while playing your mobile games or using the app. This part of the process was handled by the developers which consisted on me simply generating a code from the advertising program administrators section and emailing it to the developer. When he was finished, it was time to upload to the Google Play Store.

Uploading to The App Store

Upon receiving the.Apk file, I saved it to my computer then headed over to the Google play store developer console, which, once your account is setup, you can access this in order to manage your apps. I did get a little help uploading the files of the first app to the Google play store from the original developer because it was giving me a hard time due to the time zone differences. We used a software called Team Viewer which allows someone to remotely control your computer. It is used by a lot of companies for online meetings and to allow their tech teams to fix issues in the system remotely and can also be used free for non-commercial projects. Using this was not necessary but being that it was my first time uploading content to the app store, he went out of his way to assist me.

Once the issue was fixed with the app, it uploaded perfectly. I then was able to upload the second. Apk file that I received from the other developer by myself which I found to be very easy. I would recommend trying it out for yourself but if you are having problems, you can always ask the developer for help as they are more than likely to have a few apps in the app stores as well and can offer you help. Some developers may charge you for this but if the problem lies within the app, then they are likely to do it for free. Getting mobile apps developed and published into the app store is not as hard as many people think but there is a simple learning curve to it and as long as you can get past it, you will be fine. Don't forget to check out the book listed above which can give you great guidance to building your app.

Chapter 7. Confidentiality, Licensing, Commercial and Personal Use

In this Chapter, we will discuss a very important subject that may come up from time to time. A question that came up once I've started purchasing more Gigs on Fiverr was, "Did I own the copyright in works created by someone hired on Fiverr?" and if I did not, what are the restrictions surrounding the things I've purchased? This is a very important question because you want to own all of the creative work in your business or for your personal project— it's a major asset your brand. Also, another major question that came up was on the topic confidentiality. What if you are working on a project that involves confidential information, how can you trust that the person you are hiring doesn't disclose any information?

The best way to answer this question is to first take a look at Fiverr's Terms of Use or Terms of Service. This also goes for all other online marketplaces like, elance and oDesk (now Upwork), PeoplePerHour, Guru, Etsy or any place where you may be sourcing designs or other creative work for your business. Fiverr lays out everything we need to know about copyright ownership in their Terms of Use. At the time of writing this book, there terms around this subject states:

Ownership

Ownership and limitations: Unless clearly stated otherwise on the seller's Gig page/description, when the work is delivered, and subject to payment, the buyer is granted all intellectual property rights, including but not limited to, copyrights for the work delivered from the seller, and the seller waives any and all moral rights therein. The delivered work shall be considered work-for-hire under the U.S. Copyright Act. In the event the delivered work does not meet the requirements of work-for-hire or when US Copyright Act does not apply, the seller expressly agrees to assign to buyer the copyright in the delivered work. All transfer and assignment of intellectual property to buyer shall be subject to full payment for the Gig and the delivery may not be used if payment is canceled for any reason. For removal of doubt, in custom created work (such as artwork, design work, report generation, etc.), the delivered work shall be the exclusive property of buyer, and seller assigns all rights, title and interest in the delivered work. Some Gigs (including for custom created work) charge additional payments (through Gig Extras) for a Commercial Use License.

This means that if you purchase the Gig for personal use, you will own all rights you require for such use, and will not need the Commercial Use License. If you intend to use it for any charge or other consideration, or for any purpose that is directly or indirectly in connection with any business, or other undertaking intended for profit, you will need to buy the Commercial Use License through a Gig Extra and will have broader rights that cover your business use. Sellers further confirm that whatever information they receive from the buyer, which is not public domain, shall be kept confidential and shall not be shared or used for any purpose whatsoever other than for the delivery of the ordered work to the buyer. Furthermore, users (both buyers and sellers) agree that unless they explicitly indicate otherwise, the content users voluntarily create/upload to Fiverr, including Gig texts, photos, videos, usernames, user photos, user videos and any other information, including the display of delivered work, may be used by Fiverr for no consideration for marketing and/or other purposes.

Commercial Use License

By purchasing a "Commercial Use License" with your order, the Seller grants you a perpetual, exclusive, non-transferable, worldwide license to use the purchased delivery for Permitted Commercial Purposes. All intellectual property rights of the purchased delivery are hereby assigned to you. "Permitted Commercial Purposes" means any business-related use, such as (by way of example) advertising, promotion, creating web pages, integration into product, software or other business-related tools, etc., and strictly excludes any illegal, immoral or defamatory purpose. This License is subject to Fiverr's Terms of Service. There is no warranty, express or implied, with the purchase of this delivery, including with respect to fitness for a particular purpose. Neither the Seller nor Fiverr will be liable for any claims, or incidental, consequential or other damages arising out of this license, the delivery or your use of the delivery. In other words, unless the seller specifically states that they retain copyright ownership or they have "personal use only" restrictions then you're all good and upon payment of the Gig, you'll own all rights in the work.

Here are some quick tips to keep in mind:

Triple check the details in the Gig description page before you pay and submit your order to see if there is an add-on if you intend to use the work for business use and to see if they say anything about copyright ownership. If the seller states they retainer copyright ownership, then you have an option to keep shopping around, or If you really want to work with that seller, then see if he/she provides an add-on for transferring complete ownership. If they do, pay it. As a bonus, I also recommend taking a screenshot of the Gig page so you have a record of what was stated regarding copyright ownership on the day of your purchase. If the seller changes their rules later, you'll have proof of what you relied on when you hired him/her.

When it comes to the topic of confidentiality, as mentioned previously, there may be times when you are working on sensitive and confidential projects but you need to outsource certain tasks for whatever reasons. Let's just make it clear that it is against Fiverr's TOS to ask the person you are hiring for their name and address so signing anything like a contract is out of the question. Unless, you work with the freelancer outside of the Fiverr platform, you may be able to do this but you have to remember that Fiverr cannot be held accountable for any activity between you and the seller outside of their platform. When it comes to these type of things, buyers are protected by, again, Fiverr's TOS. Under the Non-Permitted Usage section, the Privacy & Identity restrictions state:

"You may not publish or post other people's private and confidential information. Any exchange of personal information required for the completion of a service must be provided in the order page. Sellers further confirm that whatever information they receive from the buyer, which is not public domain, shall not be used for any purpose whatsoever other than for the delivery of the work to the buyer. Any users who engage and communicate off of Fiverr will not be protected by our Terms of Service."

Under the User Conduct and Protection section, the Basic terms states:

"To protect our users' privacy, user identities are kept anonymous. Requesting or providing Email addresses, Skype/IM usernames, telephone numbers or any other personal contact details to communicate outside of Fiverr in order to circumvent or abuse the Fiverr messaging system or Fiverr platform is not permitted. Any necessary exchange of personal information required to continue a service may be exchanged within the order page. Fiverr does not provide any guarantee of the level of service offered to buyers. You may use the dispute resolution tools provided to you in the order page. Fiverr does not provide protection for users who interact outside of the Fiverr platform. All information and file exchanges must be performed exclusively on Fiverr's platform."

One thing to keep in mind is that the freelancers on Fiverr are not there to gossip or hurt your business and projects but instead they are there to work and make money. At the end of the day, none of the sellers on the platforms really wants to bring trouble upon themselves or their clients. Being professional and having a good rapport between sellers and buyers is worth the time invested. However, if confidentiality is still an issue after reading the TOS, I would advise several things. The first is to be very picky about who you choose to hire. The easiest way to find someone trustworthy is to look at the seller rating and their level. It would be best to find a highly reviewed seller who does tons of work they may have less incentive to reveal anything since they do this kind of work every day. The second piece of advice is to be creative and anonymize your work as much as possible. This can include compartmentalizing your work and order from multiple sellers that you feel good about. If you have many sellers and no one gets all of the work, you can limit the amount of knowledge that any of the sellers is privy too. I do understand that compartmentalization isn't always possible, in some cases it might be. I am sure that a certain amount of research and design could be handled that way.

Chapter 8. Important Things to Consider

Purchasing a Test Gig

The best way to a certain seller or to even test out the platform is to purchase a Test Gig. There is no Gig that is considered a "Test Gig" but the idea behind f this to find a basic Gig for $5 either from the seller you are interested in hiring or by purchasing any random Gig within your projects category. This allows you to be able to gain a basic understanding of how the entire process works on the Fiverr platform. The first puzzle app not only taught me this, but also the process of uploading your mobile app to the app store. With that information, I was able to navigate myself around and upload the second puzzle app to Google Play Store. This is essential because sometimes you will find developers who will charge you for small tasks like uploading your app to the app store.

It's Better to Spend More than $5

No one said that you can't find exceptional Gigs for $5. What you have to remember is that for that amount, you are usually getting the most basic services. For instance, if you are needing to outsource article writing or translation of a document, a $5 Gig will do just fine within those types of categories. Now if you are looking for someone to build a website, a mobile app, or something along the lines of illustrations and logos, $5 will sometimes only get you a draft or a basic page setup which will not be enough to really get you up and running. As previously mentioned in earlier chapters about the first 2 mobile apps in my portfolio, I spend more money in add-on and custom services to get the apps up and running exactly how I wanted them.

The Higher the Level of the Seller Is, The Better

When you are searching through the Gigs on Fiverr, one of my best practices is to look for high level and ranking sellers. This is not to say that I wouldn't take a chance on someone who has just posted their first freelance gig because if you can do the job then that's all that should matter. The thing is, with high level and ranking sellers, they have already proven to be successful on the platform. To get an understanding of how Fiverr promotes their sellers, basically, Level 1 sellers have been active on the site for 30 days and completed at least 10 orders while maintaining excellent ratings and a great track record. Level 2 sellers have made over 50 orders in the past two months while maintaining excellent ratings and a solid track record. Top Rated Sellers are manually chosen by Fiverr editors. Promotion is based on criteria including: seniority, volume of sales, extremely high rating, exceptional customer care and community leadership. Now although I haven't personally come across any suspicious Gigs, be aware that fake positive feedback is always a possibility with any kind of site that uses customer reviews, but you should also be aware that fake negative reviews aren't unheard of either. The best way to deal with this is communication with the person you are thinking about hiring.

Have a Clear Understanding of the Gig You Are Purchasing

It is critical that before you set out to hire someone on Fiverr by purchasing their posted Gig, you need to read the description and the job details fully so you can have a clear understanding on whether you want to hire that freelancer or not. For instance, a seller may post his or her services for a $5 minimum, but for $5, you may not get the full service that you require. This information is usually posted within the detail page and will be highlighted within the different packages, if any. Something else to look for is the orders in queue for the job you are reviewing. Orders in queue tell you how many people are ahead of you in line, a large number could mean a reduced chance of getting your gig completed early but it's also a good sign that people like the product.

Figure 5

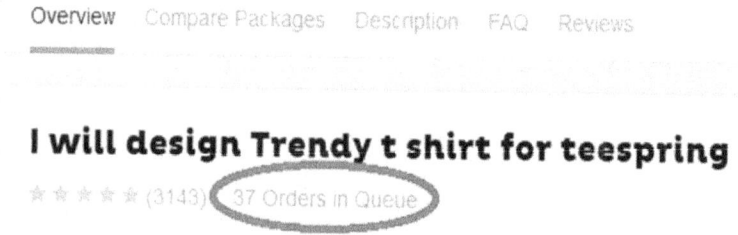

Overview Compare Packages Description FAQ Reviews

I will design Trendy t shirt for teespring

★ ★ ★ ★ ★ (3143) 37 Orders in Queue

Chapter 9. Simple Tasks that can be Outsourced on a Budget

When you discussing a topic with someone, it is always best to provide specific examples showing exactly what you are talking about. Below are real-life tasks that can be outsourced.

Simple Tasks that can be Outsourced on a Budget

Small Businesses	Virtual Administrative Assistants	Website Development	Logos & Graphics	Spokesperson & Testimonials
Authors	Book Covers	Illustrations	Proofreading & Editing	Formatting
Internet Marketers	SEO & SEM	Domain Research	Social Media Marketing	Product Listings
Musicians	Mix & Mastering	CD & Mixtape Covers	Session Musicians & Singers	a)Songwriters b) Producers c) Composers
Getting Married	Invitations & Monograms	Planning & Consulting	Video Editing	Music List Mixing
Professional Services	Accounting	Virtual Assistants	Legal Writing	a) Resumes b)Translation c) Copywriting
Medical Offices	Transcription	Data Entry	Virtual Administration Assistants	Testimonials & Endorsements
Actors & Entertainers	Headshots	Demo Reel Editing	Acting Coach	
Start Ups & Entrepreneurs	Product 3D & 2D Designs	Name & Logo Consulting	Demos & Pitch Deck	Software Design & Development
Film Directors & Producers	Voice Overs	Post Production Editing	Animated Characters & Modeling	Music Score
Realtors	Property Promo Video	Photo Editing & Retouching	Listing Descriptions	Auto CAD Drawings & 3D Models
Programming & Tech	Mobile & Web Development	User Testing	Support & IT	Database Creation
Drop Shipping Business	Product Description	Niche Research	Wholesalers & Drop shippers List	Automated Websites

Looking at the chart, you can see that there're lots of opportunities for many types of businesses and professions that can benefit from the services offered on Fiverr. While all these sites offer you the opportunity to outsource any task imaginable at a low price, that doesn't mean you should outsource it all. In fact, there are tasks that you should never outsource to sites like Fiverr or People Per Hour.

Think about it. When you've put your heart and soul into getting your site up and running, you should want to take care of it. This means that you should be hesitant to use low-cost outsourcing sites like Fiverr for work that can impact on your business brand or reputation.

One of the most common examples is link building. If you get on Fiverr.com you can quickly find users offering to build as many links to your site as you want, and for just $5. You must admit that these offers are tempting. But you'd better think twice before paying for link building gigs. As many other marketers found out the hard way, buying links on Fiverr or any other outsourcing platforms can actually be a very cheap way to kill your site's Google rankings. So try to avoid this at all costs. Here are some other tasks you should avoid outsourcing to low-cost sites like Fiverr:

Buying email lists

Thousands of contacts at only $5? That's one shortcut that tempts many business owners. But here's the truth: buying an email list is a really bad idea, and a huge waste of money. It's one of those shortcuts that simply don't work – and that may cause your business far more harm than good. There is a high chance that you'll find issues like: incorrect names, email addresses that are no longer valid or harvested from the web, where people haven't chosen to be on any list. But the consequences are even worst: you'll come across as a spammer, you'll run into trouble with your email service provider and you'll get a poor open rate. If you decide to buy email lists, expect your reputation to take a serious knock.

Buying Facebook Likes or Twitter Followers

If you buy fake fans and followers and trick people into liking your page, don't expect any results. While a massive amount of likes can give your business an impressive image at first glance, it won't help you achieve your marketing objectives – including driving engagement and sales. You might even discover that those accounts – even if they're real – are based in countries that your business doesn't operate in. So how can you expect people to click through to your website or engage with your content if they've got no interest in your brand whatsoever?

Other gigs you shouldn't outsource:

- Blog or social media shares with a huge audience
- Business plans or financial advice
- Anything that you know can't be done on the cheap
- Submission gigs (press releases, infographics, document sharing sites)

Bottom line, if you're looking to outsource tasks that have a huge impact on your brand's reputation, you might want to go with professional service providers instead.

However, sometimes you just need a small task done. For the cost of a mug of coffee, sites like Fiverr provide a way that any small business owner can reach into their own pocket, and get a webpage built, a logo designed, or a speech written. Here are some of the best services that are well suited to sites like Fiverr:

Logo designs

While a professional logo is extremely important if you're trying to build a distinctive business, there are cases when getting a logo done on the cheap makes better sense. For example, you might need a logo for a new affiliate site or a blog that you're launching. Getting one done for $5 is really helpful.

Other small design tasks

It can be anything from eBook covers to banners to infographics to backgrounds for your Twitter or Facebook pages, banner ads, image optimization and business card design. Don't waste your precious time with small design tasks when you can quickly outsource them.

YouTube transcriptions

Because no one wants to watch and transcribe an entire YouTube video. Adding the transcription to the video can help with SEO but transcribing a 30-minute video can take hours. So why not hire it out on Fiverr for a mere $5?

Foreign language translations

If you're thinking about expanding your business or running a campaign in a country where you don't speak the language, instead of paying thousands of pounds in translation costs why not get it done cheaply at Fiverr? You can even use a different gig to proofread it to ensure it's 100% accurate.

Other gigs you can outsource:

- Video editing, video introductions, voiceovers
- Simple Photoshop tasks, such as photo touchups, dropping out backgrounds and more
- Data entry, such as Excel tasks, social media scheduling, virtual assistant work
- Basic web development and troubleshooting

Chapter 9. Forming Your Outsourcing Team on Fiverr

After outsourcing your first few projects and/or task on Fiverr, by now, you should have a good feel of how the entire platform works and a simple hiring strategy in place. At this point, you may also have one or several freelancers that you've grown comfortable with and love working with. Forming relationships with freelancers on Fiverr is something you want to consider because it helps in so many ways. The trust, communication and the experience are there because of the prior times you've hired them, so working with the same freelancers makes things go much smoothly. Now let's say you have lots of constant tasks and projects to be completed on a regular basis, this can be your opportunity to start thinking about forming a virtual outsourcing team on Fiverr. A virtual team is a group of individuals who work together remotely to collaborate on a project usually communicating together via email, voice and video conferencing services, etc. Building a virtual team on Fiverr basically consist on using the same freelancers that you've already built a relationship with and individually directing their talents towards one single project, or multiple projects once you've got a strong system in place. Talking a little bit more about systems, the basis of outsourcing came because of the efficiency it provided when an ideal system is put in place. An ideal system not only includes building your virtual team but also managing your team and the tasks you've given them. The ideal system that would be put in place while building and managing a virtual outsourcing team consists on 3 main factors: Communication, Standards, and Reliability.

Communication

When building a virtual outsourcing team, communication is the key to getting the tasks that you need completed. Now while each freelancer on your team will not communicate with each other, instead you will serve as the main point of contact between you and your team. Fiverr TOS does not allow for you and the freelancer to communicate outside of their platform and if you choose too, Fiverr cannot be held liable for any damages that occur outside of the platform. With that being said, the only form of communication available will be thru Fiverr's email service. This means that the requirements of the task must be written out as clearly as possible. Any details small or large that you are requiring needs to be explained extensively so that the task can be done to your expectations. The communication between the freelancers and yourself can make or break your project and because the challenge of not being physically present together to work on the project makes things slightly difficult but not impossible. This stands true especially with projects that have intricate details but with smaller, less complex projects, lots can be accomplished within the platform.

Standards

Having a pre-formatted template that will serve as a standard outline as to what needs to be done and how it should be done can go very far. Let's say you are outsourcing articles for your new blog and you have a found a group of writers that you have already formed a business relationship with on the platform. In order for them to start researching and writing articles for the blog, giving each individual a template of how the articles should be structured will not only make it easier for you but also for the writer as well. The template should contain a short description of the details that will be included in the main heading, the introduction, the main body, any subheadings and a conclusion or ending paragraph. This will allow for the writers' research to flow smoothly which in turns helps to produce better content. Also, going into the future, the writers will know exactly how to structure your content for the blog, subsequently ending the need to explain the requirements each time you start a new article, saving both you and the writers much valuable time. Setting these types of guidelines and templates makes the entire project flow smoothly from start to finish and establishes a set of standards that can be streamlined and scaled.

Reliability

It is highly important that while you are building your virtual outsourcing team on Fiverr, that you inquire about the availability of the freelancers you are thinking about forming a team around. The freelancers on Fiverr will not solely be working on your project at one given time which means that their time may be limited, especially if they are a top seller. Nevertheless, most will still make time for your projects as most freelancers on the platform are working on multiple projects at the same time. I say this to you for you to keep in mind that if you are working on a time-sensitive project, it will be best to inquire with double the number of freelancers you will need. If you are working on a project that may require 3 freelancers, then you should inquire with 6 freelancers just as an insurance policy. In fact, this is a rule of thumb when running any business with employees, you must always hire more employees than you would need on an average day just in case someone is not available to work that day. Another option can be to inquire with the freelancer on your team ahead of time so that he or she can plan for your project around their availability. The good thing about Fiverr is the availability of the seller and the length of time it takes them to complete the order is usually posted on their profile page and under individual gig descriptions. Also, once you have submitted your order for your project, Fiverr gives their sellers a certain amount of time to complete the order using a timer that appears once you have placed your order. Needless to say, Fiverr sellers are usually good about staying on time with their orders, often times completing the orders before the due date.

Chapter 10. Top Online Outsourcing Platforms

Over the course of this book, we've talked about Fiverr in broad detail, from signing up to the platform and browsing the different gigs, examples of the gigs within Fiverr's top categories to some of the helpful tips and techniques you can use while using the platform. However, Fiverr is not the only platform you can outsource your project tasks on, there're many others that are just as unique and great to use, with some being around longer than Fiverr. Some of the other top online outsourcing platforms include Upwork, 99Designs, Guru and PeoplePerHour.

Upwork

Upwork is the world's largest online workplace, enabling businesses and freelancers to work together on-demand via the Internet. In 2015, oDesk was rebranded as Upwork. Upwork has nine million registered freelancers and four million registered clients with a total of three million jobs are posted annually. Upwork allows clients to interview, hire and work with freelancers and agencies through the company's platform in categories such as writing, web development, virtual assistance, accounting, mobile developers and more.

How It Works:

- Start by posting a job. Tell us about your project and the specific skills required.
- Upwork analyzes your needs. Our search functionality uses data science to highlight freelancers based on their skills, helping you find talent that's a good match.

- We send you a shortlist of likely candidates. You can also search our site for talent, and freelancers can view your job and submit proposals too.
- Browse profiles. View finalists' Upwork profiles to see client ratings, portfolios, Job Success scores, and more.
- Review proposals. Evaluate bids, considering each freelancer's qualifications, thought process, timeline, and overall cost.
- Schedule a chat. Ask specific questions, determine who's the best fit, and contract.
- Send and receive files. Deliver digital assets in a secure environment.
- Share feedback in real time. Use Upwork Messages to communicate via text, chat, or video.
- Simplified global payments. We deliver payments to freelancers in over 170 countries. Includes Upwork Payment Protection. Only pay for work you authorize.

99Designs

99designs is the #1 online marketplace for graphic design, including logo design, web design and other design contests. The platform has a community of more than 1,128,000 designers over 400,000 jobs completed, 33,366 designs made daily and over $150M paid to the freelance designers.

How It Works:

- Build a design brief. Tell us about your business and what you need designed. Take your time. The more details, the better your designs.
- Pick a design package. Choose the design package that's right for you. Quick tip, the larger the prize, the more designer entries you'll have.

- Launch your contest. We share your design contest with our community of more than 1,128,000 designers. From Berlin to Bombay, professional designers will brainstorm ideas just for you.

Guru

Guru.com is a freelance marketplace. It allows companies to find freelance workers for commissioned work. The platform has global network of over 1.5 million freelancers who can help with any technical, creative or business projects you have on the table. To date, Guru has over 1.5 Million members worldwide, over 1 Million jobs completed and has paid out over $200 Million to guru freelancers.

How It Works:

- Hire The Right Freelancers For The Job. Search for services being offered by freelancers that match your needs. Our global network of over 1.5 million gurus are eager to help with any technical, creative or business projects you have on the table. Explore each freelancer's profile and browse their previous work so you can hire with confidence.
- Manage Jobs From Anywhere. Keep everything on track and collaborate with your team using the Work Room. Create agreements, define milestones and tasks, communicate, and share documents without ever leaving Guru.com.
- Pay Only For A Job Well Done. Payment is simple and fast once you're satisfied with the finished product. Use SafePay for a risk-free guarantee. You pay us and we pay the freelancer only after you approve the work. It's a secure, "win-win" arrangement for both sides.

Peopleperhour

PeoplePerHour is a UK-based company whose function is as an online platform giving businesses access to thousands of skilled freelance experts in hundreds of different fields. The platform connects talented experts with savvy businesses that search for the right skills to get a Job Done quickly and with no hassle.

How It Works:

- Complete a quick form describing what you need and post your Job
- Get tons of proposals from talented experts ready to ace your project
- Select the best person and they will get your Job done!

Toptal

Toptal is an exclusive network of the top freelance software developers, designers, and finance experts in the world. The platform provides freelance software engineers and software designers to companies. Toptal enables start-ups, businesses, and organizations to hire freelancers from a growing network of top talent in the world.

How It Works:

- Tell us what kind of talent you need. What kind of talent do you need? What's your tech stack? What specific skills do you need? Submit a job to let us know what you need—the more details the better. Whether it's a single freelancer or a cross-functional team of ten, Toptal can handle it. After we get the job description, our internal team of experts will review it and connect with you to answer any questions and to get an even better understanding of your exact needs.

- We'll find you the perfect match. We'll notify you with a status report concerning your request within a few days.
- They become part of your team. We'll introduce you to your Toptal freelancer, and they'll ramp up and start working as soon as you say go. As soon as you review and sign-off on our recommended freelancer(s), they'll be ready to integrate into your team—just like an in-house employee. While Toptal talent usually works remotely, arrangements can be made to have them on-site.
- Work with them at no-risk. If you're not 100% satisfied after a trial working with a Toptal freelancer, we'll start the process all over again at absolutely no cost. Our no-risk trial period lets companies work with our talent first before deciding if they're 100% confident in moving forward. If, for whatever reason, you are not completely satisfied with a Toptal freelancer you have been paired with, you will not be liable for any payment, and we can either part ways or we will restart the entire cycle with you at absolutely no cost.

Conclusion

As pointed out in earlier chapters, with the rapid advancements of technologies, the growth of small, large and new businesses and simply, the need of people to get certain tasks completed makes outsourcing a great tool. While it is not a new practice, the new aspect of outsourcing is in how easy and affordable it has become for anyone to outsource their projects and tasks that you may not have the time or technical skills to complete. Utilizing freelance and outsourcing platforms much like Fiverr not only provide benefits to people or businesses outsourcing those jobs but it also provides a source of revenue to the freelancers providing the services. Services such as language translation, book formatting, voice-overs, creative writing and others are just some of the high demand tasks that are being outsourced daily by thousands of individuals, small teams and all size businesses.

Fiverr, like other online outsourcing marketplaces, has simplified the entire process making it easy for anyone to navigate the platform from start to finish. What has made Fiverr unique and a standout platform is the price points at which you can obtain services that would normally cost hundreds or even thousands of dollars to be rendered. For instance, Michelle has a candle business that she runs out of her home and decides that she needs a better way to organize, store and keep track of inventory. The best way for Michelle to solve this problem is to use a database management system for her business. A database management system help keeps data organized in an efficient manner that can be easily accessed by the user or administrator. Normally you can purchase a license from a software company to utilize a database that has already been created in which you just add your data. On the other hand, you can consult with a software development company who will then negotiate a price to build a custom database specifically tailored to your business. Considering both scenarios and taking into consideration factors such as the amount of space needed for data, the architecture and usability of the database, etc., this will normally cost around $1500 -$10,000. Additionally, some firms who license their database to businesses often times charge a recurring usage or maintenance fee for storing data on their servers. For a fraction of the cost, she can outsource the task to a software developer on Fiverr who can create a custom-built database management system for her business with the same quality of service as if you were spending $1500. Not leaving out the fact that in most cases, when you spend thousands of dollars on a database from a software development firm, it comes with certain benefits like on-site training and continuous technical support. In this case, it would be highly suggested that she invests some of her savings on the education of the platform that the database was built on and the system she will be using within her business. This investment will allow her to grow with the platform as her business continues to grow. Furthermore, it will also broaden her knowledge of the database and around the different aspects of her business so in the future it can be much easier to pass the knowledge down if she decides to hire employees to take over that part of the business. The opportunities that are available to you on the Fiverr platform whether you are a creative, a blogger, a business owner or just someone with an idea and a dream, are wide open for you to take advantage of. Not only does Fiverr allows you to outsource jobs for a fraction of what would normally cost hundreds and thousands of dollars, but the platform aims on delivering to their users, both sellers and buyers, quality work and a great experience.

As I conclude, it is important to know that this book was created for the sole purpose of educating, guiding and garnering awareness of anyone who may or may not know the capabilities of online outsourcing platforms like Fiverr. Outsourcing has many benefits to companies small and large, providers, government agencies, bloggers, online marketers, etc. Thousands of people all over the world have found that outsourcing is a great way of doing business because of benefits such as increasing efficiency, reduce labor cost, reduction of risk and much more. One of the top benefits comes when small businesses, especially businesses with 1 or 2 owners who run the business by themselves, start outsourcing projects that would normally be done in-house. By them outsourcing responsibilities out to freelancers, this alone frees up much valuable time, allowing the owners to focus on other core aspects of the business like gaining new clients or selling more products, etc. The key to outsourcing is to know what you want, and to ask enough questions so that both parties know exactly what is expected. Just imagine yourself owning your own business and you need to hire a few people in key areas of the business. Similar to the typical stages of the hiring process you would have in place with a day to day business, you would have in place as well when outsourcing small jobs and tasks. Selection of the candidate will probably be your biggest obstacle but nevertheless, the process is made simple on Fiverr with the sellers' portfolio available for your viewing. Just like you would review potential candidates resumes as an employer, you can view some of the previous works of a seller you are thinking about hiring. Once you've selected a few potential candidates for the job, the next step is the interview process. In this case, communication between the different sellers you have chosen as candidates needs to start with more detail information about the specific tasks that needs to be done. Once you've selected a freelancer for the job, he or she is now tasked with specific guidelines and details of the project you provided which is expected to be clear and concise. By communicating effectively from the beginning until the end, you will successful projects every time. Anybody can take advantage of the benefits that outsourcing provides. It is a viable way of doing businesses that is here to stay.

www.ingramcontent.com/pod-product-compliance
Lightning Source LLC
Chambersburg PA
CBHW070127230526
45472CB00004B/1454

* 9 7 8 1 9 8 1 1 7 6 4 2 7 *